WHY I KNOW THAT YOU DON'T LOVE YOUR CHILDREN!

What Every Parent Should Know!

Kwadw(o) Naya: Baa Ankh
Em Re A'Iyun Eil

Published by: The Golden Child Promotions Publishing Company

https://goldenchildpromotionspublishing.gold/

Scroll 2: The Fuzzy Logic Series

Published January 2022: Golden Child Promotions Publishing Ltd

PORTLAND HOUSE
BELMONT BUSINESS PARK
DURHAM
DH1 1TW.

https://goldenchildpromotionspublishing.gold/

All rights reserved. No part of this publication may be reproduced, stored in a retrieval system or transmitted in any form or by any means, electronic, mechanical, photocopying, recording, and/or otherwise without prior written permission of the publishers. This book may not be lent, resold, hired out or otherwise disposed of by way of trade in any form, binding or cover other than that in which it is published, without the prior consent of the publishers.

Don't blame anyone else, you are the only person getting in your way...be wary of distractions

– Kwadw(o) Naya: Baa Ankh Em Re A'lyun Eil

READ THIS FIRST

Download: CHOICES!
Ebook FREE!

Just to say thanks for reading my book, I would like to give you a free e-book! ($6.99 Value)
https://bookhip.com/FJVSKH

NEW RELEASE

You can get this amazing new book here:

https://goldenchildpromotionspublishing.gold/the-raising-of-the-144000-sales-page/

WHY I KNOW THAT YOU DON'T LOVE YOUR CHILDREN!

This book is the second installment of Kwadw(o) Naya: Baa Ankh Em Re A'lyun Eil's Fuzzy Logic Series. Now, we are going to delve deeper into the controversies and hidden meanings of trivial things in everyday life. By OVERstanding the full truth of this world, we will be able to form better judgments for our own and our children's futures.

This book is written in an informal style and is very informative. Kwadw(o) Naya: Baa Ankh Em Re A'lyun Eil raises concerns and issues surrounding the new digital world we live in while touching upon the lies of his past.

WHY I KNOW THAT YOU DON'T LOVE YOUR CHILDREN!

Kwadw(o) Naya: Baa Ankh
Em Re A'Iyun Eil

WHY I KNOW THAT YOU DON'T LOVE YOUR CHILDREN!

Kwadw(o) Naya: Baa Ankh
Em Re A'Iyun Eil

What is really going on in this world? Are we going backwards or forwards?

Life seems pretty strange to me—It makes no sense.

Today, I live for the future, I live for our children.

Our children are the future.

But what kind of world are we bringing them into?

I have learned so many things the hard way; please, don't make the same mistake as I did.

WHY I KNOW THAT YOU DON'T LOVE YOUR CHILDREN!

The world is changing around us; what is happening, and what can we do about it?

*Kwadw(o) Naya: Baa Ankh
Em Re A'lyun Eil*

DEDICATION

This book is dedicated to all those parents out their who **REALLY LOVE** their **CHILDREN** – the ones that **OVERSTAND** that in this **DAY** and **AGE** – **SOMETIME US PARENTS NEED TO BE CRUEL TO BE KIND**, (most often for a **GREATER GOOD**)!

CONTENTS

Dedication x

Preface xiii

Introduction xiv

Chapter 1: Educare 2

Chapter 2: Condoms 10

Chapter 3: Hiv & Aids 28

Chapter 4: Gangsta Rap—Oxymoron 40

Chapter 5: Distractions & Influences 48

Chapter 6: Social Media Addiction 58

Chapter 7A: Relationships 68

Chapter 7B: Sex 72

Chapter 8: Lies 76

Chapter 9: Religion 86

Conclusion 90

Acknowledgements 93

Afterword 95

About The Author 97

PREFACE

This book will not be popular.

Many people will not appreciate what I have to say.

Many people will not like this content.

Many people will think that I am a fool or a conspiracy nut.

But, if you do manage to read this book in its entirety, and the way you think, the way you act hasn't changed...

...then, maybe you do not **LOVE** your children? Not with **DIVINE LOVE**.

Do you know **WHAT DIVINE LOVE IS?**

Or maybe I am conspiratorial fool, who knows?

INTRODUCTION

January 11th, 2019. at 8:56 am I sat here thinking:

What is going on in this world?

What's really going on?

Don't we LOVE our children anymore?

I'm not trying to offend anyone, in any way, but how do I keep quiet?.

I've seen so many things that just don't add up and I just wonder, if you have seen the same?

We live in a day and age where everything seems to be **SDRAWKCAB**.

Does this make any sense to you? It doesn't to me

This is the year 2019, we know that.

Things should be getting better, but are they?

I really don't think so; I feel like we are sliding backwards. But that's just my humble opinion.

I am sure you will agree that the world as we know it is a strange place, but is it where we need to be? Maybe we need to move to a new world, one that would be better to our children.

It is still too much for me.

Today we have doctors that hope people get sick, lawyers that pray that people get into legal trouble, we have police waiting for people to become criminals, dentists that want tooth decay, mechanics that want our cars to break down and coffin makers who need more death.

Our teachers hope we are born silly, so they can teach us the same silliness they learned

Do people only want us to succeed so they can steal from us?

Is this the world we want to bring our children into?

It's time to ask ourselves this important question. It's time to take action!

This is just my humble opinion, and you might feel that I've completely lost my mind.

CHAPTER 1: EDUCARE

I often wonder why we send our children to school. So, let me ask you. Why do you send your children to school? Is it because you have to or because you want them to learn valuable information?

I know most parents have the best intentions, but what intentions do our schools and governments have?

That is the ultimate question.

What I realized during my school days that the level of knowledge being taught was constantly declining.

We got rid of the multiplication, long division, and complicated algebraic formulas and in with the calculator. When I was a child, I was very happy. All of my classmates were when we got calculators. Mathematics got easier overnight, we no longer had to use our brains to work things out.

Thinking about it now, I see the trap. Nowadays, I struggle to work out even the simplest sums in my head without a calculator. It may be nothing, it may be something, who knows?

What is going on with our education system?

Are children being educated or miseducated? Wouldn't they be better with **educare**?

What is education?

Let's look into the root or etymology of the word:

> *"education (n.)*
>
> 1530s, *"child-rearing,"* also *"the training of animals,"* from *Middle French* education (14c.) and directly from Latin educationem (nominative educatio) "a rearing, training," noun of action from past-participle stem of educare (see **_educate_**). Originally of instruction in social codes and manners; meaning "systematic schooling and training for work" is from the 1610s.

All education is despotism. [William Godwin, "Enquirer," 1797]"[1]

Now let's look at the meaning:

"**Education** is the process of facilitating learning, or the acquisition of knowledge, skills, values, beliefs, and habits. Educational methods include storytelling, discussion, teaching, training, and directed research."[2]

Education is not fit for our children. It's all about training, instruction, storytelling, and direction. Where is nurturing, caring, and support?

From the 1530s to the 1610s, education related to child rearing and the training of animals was systematic schooling, training children to become workers. Nothing has changed today.

If this is the case, this system is not for me or my children. They need Educare, not just education, and I have to find a way to give them what they

---

[1] https://www.etymonline.com/word/education#etymonline_v_29710 accessed 13th Jan 2019 @ 07:02

[2] https://en.wikipedia.org/wiki/Education accessed 16th Jan 2019 @ 01:28

really need. I have divine love for those I hold close. That love is greater than any other, even that which I have for myself.

Most of you reading this will still be sending your children to school. What else can you do? How did you carry on with you life?

Life is about choices and we all need to make ours.

While we have just been living our lives, what's happening to our babies?

So what is educare?

> According to "Century Dictionary," educare, of a child, is usually with reference to bodily nurture or support, while educare refers more frequently to the mind, and, ***"There is no authority for the common statement that the primary sense of education is to 'draw out or unfold the powers of the mind.'"***

Is it possible that the poor in our society are receiving education while the rich are benefitting from educare?

What is your purpose in life?

Does your child know what their purpose is? Do they have any idea what kind of impact they will have on the world?

Do you know where you're going in life? Do you know what you want to be? Do your children?

Do you know anything about the achievements of our ancestors?

We all need **direction** and **goals.** Today is an important day to concentrate on your direction, on your goals. Remember, tomorrow never comes.

It never comes...

I'm not here to teach parents how to 'suck eggs' but I know that mothers and fathers do not get the information that we need in order to make informed decisions. If you don't have children, it is even better that you are reading this.

So many of us are on the road to nowhere.

Our lack of direction stems from the lack of knowledge, information, and understand that was imposed upon us and our parents.

Are you still with me? What can we do?

Well, we can work, as families, on collective solutions. We can bring back the community, the common unity we all need.

What has happened to our communities of old? We used to have so much power.

HOW MUCH DO WE LOVE OUR CHILDREN?

It is not for me to judge I know, but this is one of the questions that we parents need to ask ourselves, you may not agree.

I believe, as parents, we need to do the right thing for our children. We need to do the most beneficial thing we can, not the most popular or prescribed, but the correct action in any situation.

We all know children don't always know what's best for them. They may know what they want, but not what they need.!

We also know that no one cares more about our children than we do.

Here are some things we haven't been teaching our children that they need to know:

- Leadership
- Wealth Creation
- Wealth Building
- True History
- Creativity and The Power of The Mind
- Business and Job Creation
- Peace, Service, Unity, and Divine Love

What is your take on all of this?

CHAPTER 2: CONDOMS

I should have a lot of love for my parents.

But I have hate!

It is not their fault! Or is it?

When I was a lad, I was told to wear condoms all the time. My mother said it, so did my father, aunties, uncles, society and the media; everyone was saying wear condoms.

They said condoms meant safe sex, to protect us from disease and unwanted pregnancy.

This made no sense to me.

You must be thinking, he's just a pessimist. Never happy, always picking holes in everything. Or... you're thinking I'm crazy.

I'm sorry if you see me this way, but I beg you, to keep listening.

I think that condoms were actually meant to reduce the population of '**OUR 'WORLDS'** not to protect from diseases but promote unadulterated sex.

> **_unadulterated_**
>
> **Meaning**:
>
> Without qualification; used informally as (often pejorative) intensifiers"[3]

Sex was sacred in ancient society, they used to respect culture and respect life.. They used to live by way of the ankh, not the cross. Most relationships in ancient times lasted until death and chidlren did not have sex until marriage, which was facilitated and nurtured by both families. There were no diseases, no one slept around, and relationships used to last.

Our ancestors had a great system; why can we not bring that back? Wouldn't it be so much better than the system we have now?

Look back, see how much smoother things were back then. We should be more forward thinking than our ancestors, we should have furthered the knowledge that they left for us, but it seems that we are going **SDRAWKCAB?**

Let us take a look at how:

---

[3] https://www.audioenglish.org/dictionary/unadulterated.htm accessed 13th Jan 2019 @ 15:03

"Program: Condom Promotion and Distribution to Prevent HIV/AIDS

A note on this page's publication date

The content on this page has not been recently updated. This content is likely to be no longer fully accurate, both with respect to the research it presents and with respect to what it implies about our views and positions.

Published: 2009

In a nutshell

Problem: HIV/AIDS is one of the leading killers of adults worldwide. The virus weakens the immune system and ultimately leads to death.

Program: Condom promotion, through education, counselling, and advertising, encourages the use of condoms. Condom distribution makes condoms readily available to individuals either for free or at highly subsidised prices.

Track record: Condoms effectively prevent HIV transmission through sexual intercourse. The effectiveness of condom promotion and distribution programs is less clear.

Cost-effectiveness: Condom promotion can be highly cost-effective, estimated as preventing a case of HIV/AIDS for $550-2,240, but costs vary widely with the specific type of program implemented.

Bottom line: Condom promotion and distribution is effective at preventing HIV infections, under the right conditions. However, the lack of a strong evidence base for this approach implies that donors should require relatively strong monitoring and evaluation from a charity working on this type of **program**."4

"Condom

"A condom is a sheath-shaped barrier device, used during sexual intercourse to reduce the probability of pregnancy or a sexually transmitted infection. There are both male and female condoms. With proper use—and use at every act of intercourse—women whose partners use male condoms experience a 2% per year pregnancy rate." More at Wikipedia

Type: Barrier

First use: Ancient, Rubber: 1855, Latex: 1920s,

---

4 https://www.givewell.org/international/technical/programs/condom-distribution accessed 13th Jan 2019 @ 15:08

> **Polyurethane:** 1994, Polyisoprene: 2008"[5]
>
> "Condom - Wikipedia

You can see here as most of us know that condoms are not a bad thing... but is that the truth?

> **"ISSUES AND IMPLICATIONS**
>
> *Public Health Advocates Say Campaign to Disparage Condoms Threatens STD Prevention Efforts*
>
> **Heather D. Boonstra**, *Guttmacher Institute*
> *First published online: March 1, 2003*
>
> In 1999, social conservatives in Congress initiated a new strategy to further their moral agenda of promoting abstinence outside of marriage as official government policy—claiming that condoms do not protect against sexually transmitted diseases (STDs). Led by then-Rep. Tom Coburn (R-OK), a physician and staunch pro-abstinence opponent of government-funded family planning programs, they were successful in attaching an amendment to the House version of the Breast and Cervical Cancer Treatment Act, mandating that condom packages carry a cigarette-type warning that condoms offer "little or no protection" against an extremely common STD, human papillomavirus (HPV), some strains of which cause cervical cancer. Although this directive was removed before the bill was enacted, Coburn and his allies were able to secure a requirement that the Food and Drug Administration (FDA) re-examine condom labels to determine whether they are medically accurate with respect to condoms'

---

5   https://duckduckgo.com/?q=condoms&t=h_&ia=web accessed 13th Jan 2019 @ 15:40

"effectiveness or lack of effectiveness" in STD prevention. They also were instrumental in convincing the National Institutes of Health (NIH)—along with the U.S. Agency for International Development (USAID), the FDA and the Centers for Disease Control and Prevention (CDC)—to convene a workshop in June 2000 to evaluate published evidence on condom effectiveness.

At the time, Coburn's anti-condom views were widely considered extreme. Certainly, they were, and continue to be, out of step with mainstream public health prevention efforts. But in the intervening few years, the political landscape has changed radically. Coburn and like-minded colleagues are now ensconced within the Bush administration, and with the imprimatur of government and the report of an NIH workshop on condom effectiveness to cite, a campaign to disparage the value of condom use is in full swing, itself the cornerstone of an effort to undermine the very notion of sexual risk-reduction, or "safer sex."

Critics in the HIV and STD prevention communities worry that the conservative crusade to promote abstinence outside of marriage comes at too high a cost. Undermining people's confidence in the effectiveness of condoms threatens people's health and even lives, they argue, since sex among unmarried people is common in the United States and around the world, and achieving correct and consistent condom use is difficult enough. Moreover, they insist, condom critics are selectively citing and intentionally misrepresenting findings from the NIH workshop report to buttress their case; **the conclusion that correct condom use does not offer a high degree of protection against the vast majority of STDs, not to mention HIV and unintended pregnancy, is simply not warranted by the science, they say.**"[6]

---

6   https://www.guttmacher.org/gpr/2003/03/public-health-advocatessay-campaign-disparage-condoms-threatens-std-prevention-efforts accessed 13th Jan 2019 @ 15:17

National Security Study Memorandum

NSSM 200

Implications of Worldwide Population Growth
For U.S. Security and Overseas Interests
(THE KISSINGER REPORT)

December 10, 1974

CLASSIFIED BY Harry C. Blaney, III
SUBJECT TO GENERAL DECLASSIFICATION SCHEDULE
OF EXECUTIVE ORDER 11652 AUTOMATICALLY DOWN-
GRADED AT TWO YEAR INTERVALS AND DECLASSIFIED
ON DECEMBER 31, 1980.

This document can only be declassified by the White House.

Declassified/Released on 7/3/89
under provisions of E.O. 12356
by F. Graboske, National Security Council

"Exposing the Global Population Control Agenda

By Brian Clowes, Ph.D.

The Formalization of United States Population Policy
The United States National Security Council is the highest decision-making body on foreign policy in the United States. On December 10, 1974, it promulgated a top-secret document entitled "National Security Study Memorandum or NSSM-200," also called "The Kissinger Report." Its subject was "Implications of Worldwide Population Growth for U.S. Security and Overseas Interests." This document, published shortly after the first major international population conference in Bucharest, was the result of collaboration among the Central Intelligence Agency (CIA), the United States Agency for International Development (USAID), and the Departments of State, Defense, and Agriculture.

The Kissinger Report was made public when it was declassified and was transferred to the U.S. National Archives in 1990.

Although the United States government has issued hundreds of policy papers dealing with various aspects of American national security since 1974, The Kissinger Report continues to be the foundational document on population control issued by the United States government. It, therefore, continues to represent official United States policy on population control and is **posted on the USAID website**.

NSSM-200 is critical to pro-life workers all over the world because it completely exposes the unsavory and unethical motivations and methods of the population control movement.

The Purpose of The Kissinger Report

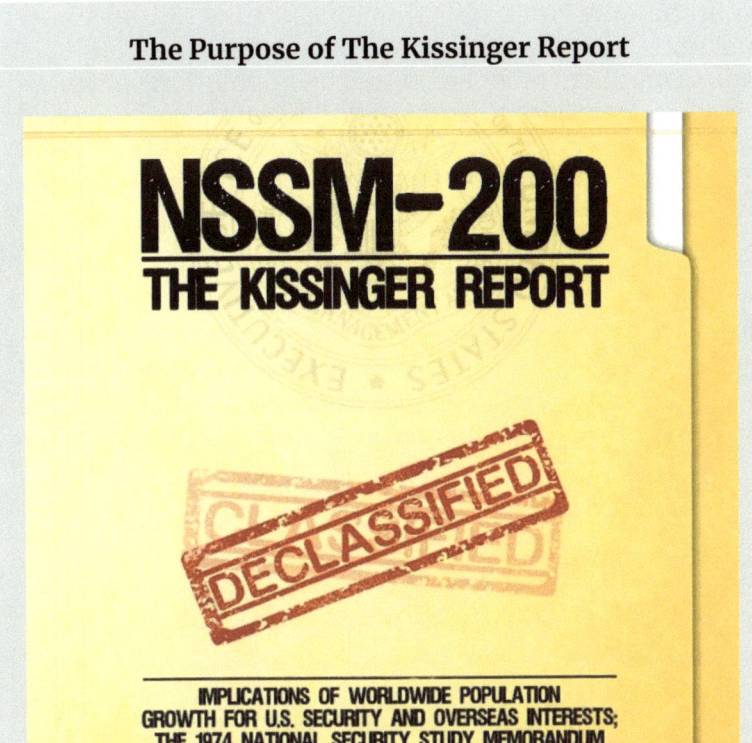

The primary purpose of U.S.-funded population control efforts is to maintain access to the mineral resources of less-developed countries, or LDCs. The Kissinger Report says that the U.S. economy will require large and increasing amounts of minerals from abroad, especially from less developed countries. That gives the U.S. enhanced interest in the political, economic, and social stability of the supplying countries. Wherever a lessening of population pressures through reduced birth rates can increase the prospects for such stability, population policy becomes relevant to the economic interests of the United States.

In order to protect U.S. commercial interests, NSSM-200 cited a number of factors that could interrupt the smooth flow of materials from LDCs to the United States, including a large population of anti-imperialist youth, whose numbers must be limited by population control. The document identified 13 nations, by name. that would be the primary targets of U.S.-funded population control efforts. Under the heading of "Concentration on Key Countries" we find:

"Assistance for population moderation should give primary emphasis to the largest and fastest growing developing countries where there is special U.S. political and strategic interest. Those countries are: India, Bangladesh, Pakistan, Nigeria, Mexico, Indonesia, Brazil, the Philippines, Thailand, Egypt, Turkey, Ethiopia and Columbia [sic]. ... At the same time, the U.S. will look to the multilateral agencies, especially the U.N. Fund for Population Activities which already has projects in over 80 countries to increase population assistance on a broader basis with increased U.S. contributions. **This is desirable in terms of U.S. interests and necessary in political terms in the United Nations.**"

According to The Kissinger Report, implementation of population control programs could include:

- The legalization of abortion.
- Financial incentives for countries to increase their abortion, sterilization, and contraception use
- Indoctrination of children.
- Mandatory population control and other forms of coercion, such as withholding disaster funds and food aid unless an LDC implements population control programs.

The Kissinger Report also specifically stated that the United States was to cover up its population control activities and avoid charges of imperialism by enlisting the United Nations and various non-governmental organizations—specifically the Pathfinder Fund, the International Planned Parenthood Foundation (IPPF), and the Population Council—to do its dirty work.

Cause of Massive Human Rights Violations

The document has directly and inevitably encouraged atrocities on an enormous scale in dozens of nations. Just four examples are shown below.

- **China:** For many years, the United States government funded the United Nations Population Fund (UNFPA). In April 2017, *the Trump Administration finally took the step of ending UNFPA funding.* Why? One of the main targets of UNFPA money was the People's Republic of China (PRC). The State Department grounded the change of policy the fact the agency "supports, or participates in the management of, a program of coercive abortion or involuntary sterilization" in China. While the UNFPA denies it, according to its own documents, *they have donated more than $100 million to China's population control program*; financed a $12 million computer complex specifically to monitor the program; provided the technical expertise and personnel that trained thousands of Chinese population control officials; and presented China with a United Nations award for the "most outstanding population control program." Those unfamiliar with the countless abuses perpetrated under this program might consider reading material from 2015-present on the links between the *U.S. Congressional Hearing on China* and *Population Research Institute* (PRI) for evidence. As the PRI article states, "More children were aborted under the one-child policy than the entire population of the United States."

- **Peru:** During the years 1995 to 1997, *over a quarter of a million Peruvian women were sterilized* as part of a program to fulfil then-president Alberto Fujimori's family planning goals. Although this was called the "Voluntary Surgical Contraception Campaign," many of these procedures were obviously coerced. In fact, women whose underweight children were on government food programs were threatened with the withholding of this aid if they refused to be sterilized, and others were kidnapped from their families and forcibly sterilized.

- **Uganda:** Uganda became the first African country to roll back its adult HIV infection rate, from 21 percent in 1991 to about 6 percent in 2004, a 70 percent decrease. The nation accomplished this amazing feat *by discouraging condom use and by changing the behavior of the people*. The population control groups could not allow this success to interfere with their inflexible template, so they aggressively undermined President Yoweri Museveni's program. Timothy Wirth, President of the United Nations Foundation, called this highly effective program a "gross negligence toward humanity." The United States Agency for International Development (USAID), Population Services International, CARE International, and others have been pushing condoms as hard as they can in Uganda. Rates rose over 7 percent which Edward Greene, former senior research scientist at the Harvard School of Public Health, *ascribes to riskier behavior* and less fear of HIV as a death sentence. *Recently rates have declined back to 6.2 percent again.* Nevertheless, Uganda's initial success rate is perhaps the most egregious example of population control ideology trumping the science of proven HIV prevention programs.

- **India:** In 2014, there was renewed international attention on India's continuing forced sterilization program after *dozens of women were killed* and many more harmed due to the *grotesquely unsanitary conditions* in factories. Female sterilization is still India's primary method of "contraception." According to the New York Times, as of 2016, four million tubal ligations were done annually. This continues to be financed by the *US and other Western governments and foundations*. As of 2017, there are no plans to stop sterilizations, but the Indian government is *introducing free injectable contraceptives*, which will also have major negative impacts on women's health.

Outline of the Population Control Strategy in The Kissinger Report:

The Kissinger Report explicitly lays out a detailed strategy by which the United States government aggressively promotes population control in developing nations. in order to regulate (or have better access to) the natural resources of these countries.

The following is an outline of this plan, with actual supporting quotes from *NSSM-200*:

The United States needs widespread access to the mineral resources of less-developed nations (quote shown above).

The smooth flow of resources to the United States could be jeopardized by LDC government action, labor conflicts, sabotage, or civil disturbances, which are much more likely if population pressure is a factor: "These types of frustrations are much less likely under conditions of slow or zero population growth."

Young people are much more likely to challenge imperialism and the world's power structures, so their numbers should be kept down as much as possible: "These young people can more readily be persuaded to attack the legal institutions of the government or real property of the 'establishment,' 'imperialists,' multinational corporations, or other—often foreign—influences blamed for their troubles."

Therefore, the United States must develop a commitment to population control among key LDC, while bypassing the will of their people: "The U.S. should encourage LDC leaders to take the lead in advancing family planning and population stabilization both within multilateral organizations and through bilateral contacts with other LDCs."

The critical elements of population control implementation include:

Identifying the primary targets: "Those countries are: India, Bangladesh, Pakistan, Nigeria, Mexico, Indonesia, Brazil, the Philippines, Thailand, Egypt, Turkey, Ethiopia, and Colombia." Enlisting the aid of as many multilateral population control organizations as possible in this worldwide project, in order to deflect criticism and charges of imperialism: "The U.S. will look to the multilateral agencies, especially the U.N. Fund for Population Activities, which already has projects in over 80 countries to increase population assistance on a broader basis with increased U.S. contributions."

Recognizing that "No country has reduced its population growth without resorting to abortion."

Designing programs with financial incentives for countries to increase their abortion, sterilization, and contraception-use rates: "Pay women in the LDCs to have abortions as a method of family planning. ... Similarly, there have been some controversial, but remarkably successful, experiments in India, in which financial incentives, along with other motivational devices were used to get large numbers of men to accept vasectomies."

Concentrating on "indoctrinating" [NSSM-200's language] the children of LDCs with anti-natalist propaganda: "Without diminishing in any way the effort to reach these adults, the]focus of attention should be to change the attitudes of the next generation, those who are now in elementary school or younger."

Designing and instigating propaganda programs and sex-education curricula intended to convince couples to have smaller families, regardless of social or cultural considerations: "The following areas appear to contain significant promise in effecting fertility declines and are discussed in subsequent sections...concentrating on the education and indoctrination of the rising generation of children regarding the desirability of smaller family size."

Investigating the desirability of mandatory [NSSM-200's language] population control programs: "The conclusion of this view is that mandatory programs may be needed and that we should be considering these possibilities now."

- Consider using coercion in other forms, such as withholding disaster and food aid unless a targeted LDC implements population control programs: "On what basis should such food resources then be provided? Would food be considered an instrument of national power? Will we be forced to make choices as to whom we can reasonably assist, and if so, should population efforts be a criterion for such assistance?"

- Throughout the implementation process, the United States must hide its tracks and disguise its programs as altruistic:

"There is also the danger that some LDC leaders will see developed country pressures for family planning as a form of economic or racial imperialism; this could well create a serious backlash ... The U.S. can help to minimize charges of an imperialistic motivation behind its support of population activities by repeatedly asserting that such support derives from a concern with:

The right of the individual couple to determine freely and responsibly the number and spacing of children, to have information, education, and means to do so; and The fundamental social and economic development of poor countries in which rapid population growth is both a contributing cause and a consequence of widespread poverty."

The Basic Question: Is Population Control Necessary?"[7]

---

7 https://www.hli.org/resources/exposing-the-global-populationcontrol/ accessed 13th Jan 2019 @ 15:03

The full article was publicly available at the website address highlighted at foot note seven (on 13th Jan 2021) but most recently it is now showing as unavailable - check for YOUR-SELF and YOU will SEE.

After reading all of this I am not sure what to think, everywhere you look there seems to be a flood of information. Surely our governments) would not deceive us?

What do you think?

CHAPTER 3: HIV & AIDS

Kwadw(o) Naya: Baa Ankh Em Re A'lyun Eil

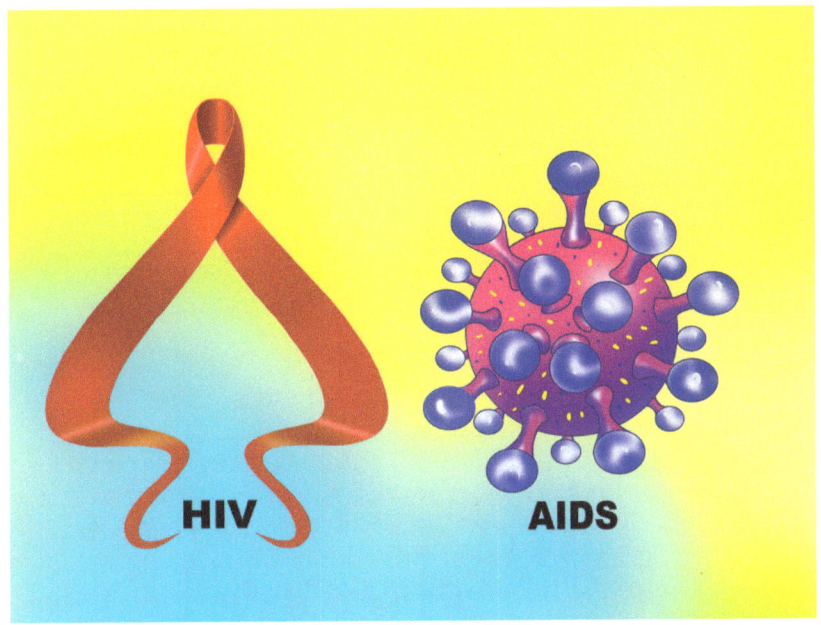

The truth is often hard to find, that I know!

This is the official story from the government website:

> **"What is HIV and AIDS?"**
>
> HIV is a virus spread through certain body fluids that attack the body's immune system, specifically the CD4 cells orT cells. Over time, HIV can destroy so many of these cells that the body can't fight off infections or disease. Untreated, HIV reduces the number of CD4 cells in the body. This damage to the immune system makes it harder and harder for the body to fight off infections and other diseases. Opportunistic infections or cancers take advantage of a very weak immune system and signal that

the person has AIDS. Learn more about the stages of HIV and how to know if you're infected.

What is HIV?

HIV stands for Human Immunodeficiency Virus. It is the virus that can lead to Acquired Immune DeficiencySyndrome, or AIDS, if not treated. Unlike some other viruses, the human body can't get rid of HIV completely, even with treatment. So, once you get HIV, you have it for life.

No effective cure currently exists, but with proper medical care HIV can be controlled. The medicine used to treat HIV is called *antiretroviral therapy* or ART. If taken the right way, every day, this medicine can dramatically prolong the lives of people infected with HIV, keep them healthy, and greatly lower their chance of infecting others. Before the introduction of ART in the mid-1990s, people with HIV could progress to AIDS in just a few years. Today, a person being effectively treated for HIV can live nearly as long as someone who does not have HIV.

What is AIDS?

AIDS is the most severe phase of HIV infection. The immune systems of people with AIDS cannot fight off any attack, meaning that they get an increasing number of severe illnesses, called *opportunistic infections*." [8]

Please see also:

---

[8] https://www.hiv.gov/hiv-basics/overview/about-hiv-and-aids/whatare-hiv-and-aids accessed 17th Jan 2019 @ 22:29

> *AIDS and **HIV** Health Center – WebMD*
>
> Human Immunodeficiency Virus, or **HIV**, is the virus that causes AIDS. **HIV** weakens a person›s ability to fight infections. It is often contracted through unprotected sex or needle sharing."9

It seems to be the same story you see everywhere. Most mainstream, or even 'any stream' media is saying the same.

Don't you think this life is funny?

Please check out the following extracts from a very interesting report written by Stefan Lanka in 1996. It highlights some important details, issues, and even contrasting views among experts.

> **"RETHINKING HIV:**
>
> Collective Fallacy"
>
> By Stefan Lanka
>
> Continuum Sept./Oct. 1996
>
> "It is a dire example of how a distinguished scholar who has contributed much to the advancement of science, now

---

9   https://www.webmd.com/hiv-aids/default.htm accessed 17th Jan 2019 @ 2:36

impedes further progress by his stubborn adherence to a dogma of his own creation. If he did not feel himself obliged to repeat things, that are untrue just because they were once said, they would have become quite different people.
- Johann Wolfgang von Goethe, Maximen und Reflexionen, Texstelle 586."

"Readers will be aware that there have been a number of claims for, and responses to, Continuum's offer of a reward for "The missing Virus." These have ranged from requests for clarification as to the type of proof required, through dismissive comments that the proof sought was an irrelevance, to an outright claim to the prize by Professor Peter Duesberg. Readers will recall that the point of the whole exercise was consistent with my article explaining that HIV does not actually exist, as opposed to the more frequently asked question whether HIV is responsible for AIDS or not.

The distinguished Australians led by Dr Eleopulos-Papadopolus have already provided a detailed reply to the Duesberg claim, so I shall endeavour to explain how the erroneous concept of retroviruses brought about the present situation.

Duesberg's enormous services to mankind are beyond dispute. It is he who for nearly 10 years now, has steadfastly and at great personal cost, been the anchor of sanity and decency in a world driven mad by the simple-minded HIV theory. Whether HIV exists and whether it causes AIDS is largely academic: when did you last come across a "normal" heterosexual-someone who does not derive his living from perpetuating the panic-who takes the slightest notice personally of the official story? In practice, Duesberg's claim to our unqualified gratitude has been his long standing and unwavering opposition to AZT (and its analogues), whose use always ends in death.

That said, it is unfortunately also true that Duesberg is himself the victim of another collective fallacy (the Denkkollektiv of Ludwig Fleck), which he himself helped to formulate and which he is now apparently locked into"

CONCLUSION

The rules demonstrating the existence of HIV (and retroviruses in general) were never validated or adhered to by those who devised them. It makes sense that people asked this magazine what the 'isolation' meant: suitable synonyms might be 'pure' and/or 'free of contaminants.' Readers were clearly concerned that the term was used in retrovirology rather as in Alice in Wonderland, "it means what I say it means."

Until AIDS was invented, retro-virologists were a minority sect who were happy to accept the theories of others without much speculation. They could fiddle around to their hearts' content, safe in the knowledge that "retroviruses were the least dangerous of all viruses." Well-meaning and credulous colleagues, as well as aspiring virologists, journalists and, through them, laymen were mesmerized by incomprehensible jargon. Each property relating to HIV, and retroviruses in general, can be shown to pertain to the cells used in the co-cultivation experiments. There is no reason to think that these properties and components have anything to do with viruses in general, nor with "HIV" in particular.

NO PARTICLE OF HIV HAS EVER BEEN OBTAINED PURE, FREE OF CONTAMINANTS; NOR HAS A COMPLETE PIECE OF HIV RNA (OR THE TRANSCRIBED DNA) EVER BEEN PROVED TO EXIST. *" [10]

The full report is available on the link below (footnote 10).

What do you think?

Did you manage to pick up the key pointers?

---

10   http://virusmyth.com/aids/hiv/slreplypd.htm acessed 21st Jan 2019 @ 22:57

First, there are the words of *Johann Wolfgang von Goethe*, did you take note?

I also noticed a couple of other statements which triggered a reaction in my head, please see:

> "Until AIDS was **invented**, retrovirologists were a minority sect who were happy to accept each others' flights of fancy without being too critical."

Until AIDS was invented? What is this? He said it was invented; if true, that's awful. He is probably crazy. just like me. I guess some people can look into things too much. I don't know. What are your thoughts? Maybe we should all look into some of this stuff? What do you think?

The final statement of this report is the most concerning to me. I have heard many experts speak out about this, but not publicly or on mainstream media.

Please see the extract below:

> "NO PARTICLE OF HIV HAS EVER BEEN OBTAINED PURE, FREE OF CONTAMINANTS; NOR HAS A COMPLETE PIECE OF HIV RNA (OR THE TRANSCRIBED DNA) EVER BEEN PROVED TO EXIST."

All is not what it seems, I am sure that many of you will agree.

I have heard quite a few top-level experts say that HIV does not exist, but we have also heard almost everywhere that it does? Which one is it? Maybe we have all been spun lies, mistakes have been made somewhere, or maybe just an advancement in biological sciences and medicine is required. New information always takes a while to come out. I know. Look at Edison and Tesla. they both thought they knew best. Tesla with his A.C. (alternating current) electricity and Edison with his D.C. (direct current electricity).

One man was right, and the other was not so right, one man had plenty of money while the other man had next to none.

Which electricity did the government and all the rich corporations back? Which electricity was rolled out across America, only to be replaced at a later date with its competitor?

I am sure you know the rest of the story, if not I suggest you check it out. It may open your eyes a little and you may think that the methodology behind all this stuff is the same. Strange coincidental, maybe I am looking into things too much.

What do you think?

I have heard that AIDS come from monkeys, Africa, homosexuals, and even from unprotected sex. They say that HIV nearly always develops into full blow AIDS.

But the funny thing is, experts say that AIDS was invented in a lab?

I don't know what's going on anymore, do you?

Who do you trust?

The government or the experts?

I am no expert, so I don't really know but I am a parent and all these things are quite worrying to me.

What are your thoughts on all of this, I would be very interested to know.

What do you think?

Before you leave this chapter, I would like to leave you with a couple of short extracts which are very intriguing:

> "**The Deadly Fallacy of the HIV-AIDS-Death Hypothesis: Exposing the Epidemic that Is Not** by Mwizenge S. Tembo 1, Ph. D. Associate Prof. of Sociology Bridgewater College "We cannot live without sex," ...."What else is there, where is the enjoyment? We might

as well be dead." - National Geographic, April 1988 - a man in a village living a hard existence of daily physical chores in Rakai in Uganda when told that the AIDS epidemic was contracted through sex.

ABSTRACT

The paper describes the basic tenet of the HIV-AIDS-equals-to-death hypothesis and the major controversy surrounding the disease. Second, the paper challenges the validity and reliability of the HIV-AIDS-equals-to-death hypothesis. It is argued that this possible erroneous hypothesis has been maintained and in some cases ruthlessly protected and used as the impetus or linch pin for driving national and international public health policy. The third objective explores the positive and negative real life implications and outcomes for science and public health in Western and non-Western societies in clinging on to and promoting a possibly severely flawed HIV-AIDS-equals-to-death hypothesis. The paper concludes with recommendations on what science, Zambians and perhaps the public should do to investigate, counteract, correct, and if possible remove the illegitimate and perhaps scandalous influence of the HIV-AIDS orthodoxy."

"It was and is wrong to tell people they are carrying a deadly new virus on the basis of an unvalidated test, beset with technical problems and pitfalls in interpretation, vulnerable to shipping, climatic and storage conditions, and subject to unmeasured and probably immeasurable cross-reactivities and hence false positive results. It is very hard for doctors, scientists, politicians, the World Health Organization, gay leaders, Aids charities and even journalists to admit to this today, since they have all been instrumental in bringing about the climate of opinion in which this unvalidated test was inflicted on millions. But those are the facts. Regardless of whether or not the test has any relevance to a retrovirus, there are so many other possible causes of a positive result that on present knowledge, no one should be diagnosed as suffering from 'HIV' infection or disease. No one cognizant of these facts will ever wish to allow themselves to be tested. The sooner the error is acknowledged, and the test relegated to history, the quicker we may see a return to sanity in Aids science."(Hodgkinson, 1996:262)" [11]

There's not much more to say, what are your thoughts?

---

[11] https://wp.bridgewater.edu/mtembo/wpcontent/uploads/sites/380/2016/11/HIVAIDSPaper-1.pdf accessed 17th Jan 2019 @ 23:19

CHAPTER 4:
GANGSTA RAP-OXYMORON

Here I talk about the music industry and the media.

It takes so much time from us and our children.

What a distraction!

It would be great if they set a good example for us to follow but that is rarely the case.

I look at gangsta rap because it used to inspire me when I was a child. It used to be my favourite music, just like American wrestling was my favourite sport.

Now, I love neither, and my heart is broken.

Why?

Because, at 42 years old, almost everything I was taught is a lie.

Gangsta rap is a lie, wrestling is a lie, global warming is a lie, Brexit is a lie, even Santa and the 'bleeding' **TOOTH FAIRY** are lies!

Why I Know That You Do Not Love Your Children!

So, we have poetic gangsterism (I take it) or gangtsa poetry. :o) How can this be?

Please check out the following:

(1) "DMX: "BRING YA WHOLE CREW"

Via: www.dmxtour.com

This was the second song on the sophomore album titled Flesh of my Flesh, Blood of my Blood by the Yonkers rapper DMX. He was feeling very violent on this one and his aggression spilled all over the record. *In one part of the song, he talks about having "blood on his d***," because "he f***ed a corpse." Elsewhere he says, "I'm bout to find out how much guts you got before I spill 'em."* Seems like someone was having a very bad day.

(2) CAGE – "BALLAD OF WORMS"

Via: www.deviantart.com

Sometimes rappers are able to tap into the sickest thoughts that human beings could ever think of. And that's what Cage did with the track "Ballad of Worms." In the song, he talks about caring for his dying girlfriend and he gets really graphic and raw. Some of the lyrics include, "Can't stop what's hurting her / No sleep with her screaming all night, I'm thinking of murking her / Her parents paid for the coffin and left state / After signing the contract, do not resuscitate." It gets even sicker than that—check this song out for yourselves.

(3) GETO BOYS – "CHUCKIE"

Via: www.mtvhive.com

One of the pioneers of the gangsta rap scene in 1991 was the group Geto Boys consisting of Scarface, Willie D, and Bushwick Bill. They were known for their unfiltered and twisted lyrics. One of those songs was called "Chuckie" and the lyrics are quite disgusting. One of the opening lines rapped by Bushwick Bill was: "That's why I murdered your nieces / wasn't my fault they found their heads cut in 88 pieces." Wow, that's some very heavy, dark material.

(4) EMINEM – "STAN"

Via: vbox7.com

One of the most descriptive narrative songs ever released in rap is the 1999 song called "Stan" by Detroit rapper *Eminem*. The song features the rapper in rare storytelling form talking about a disturbed fan penning him in a letter. The song culminates with this disillusioned rapper putting his pregnant girlfriend in the trunk of his car and crashing over a bridge into the water below. One of the most disturbing lines in the song was: "But I didn't slit her throat, I just tied her up / See I ain't like you / Cause if she suffocates she'll suffer more and then she'll die too."

(5) NECRO – "DEAD BODY DISPOSAL"

Via: m3event.wordpress.com

When it comes to the horrorcore genre of rap, there's no rapper who is more terrifying and twisted than the 38-yr-old Brooklyn rapper known as Necro. For over a decade, he has been putting out some of the most disturbing songs. One track is called "Dead Body Disposal." From the opening lines of the song, it's immediately apparent that Necro's mind is extremely dark. He raps "Let's talk about dead body disposal, take the corpse to the bathtub and drain the blood out of the bastard." Someone get this guy a shrink please.[12]

---

12 https://www.therichest.com/rich-list/most-shocking/the-11-most-violent-and-disturbing-rap-songs/ accessed 13th Jan 2019 @ 16:49

I know we all have freedom of speech, but what is this?

Often the music is catchy, a proper ear worm.

I ask you now once again, what is this?

This is part of the reason why I don't listen to Gangsta Rap music. The other part, the main part is because of the lies

I know gangsters, real gangsters.

And you know what...

TRUE GANGSTERS NEVER TALK!

We all should know that.

It seems that most of my idols were toy gangsters, which is why I no longer listen to their music.

I no longer worship these puppets, and neither will my children!

CHAPTER 5: DISTRACTIONS & INFLUENCES

Kwadw(o) Naya: Baa Ankh Em Re A'lyun Eil

I remember life being simple when I was a child

Now, I don't feel as if I can say the same. There are far too many (external) distractions and influences (not always positive).

Shouldn't things be a lot simpler with all the technology we have?

But are they?

My main motto in life (love aside) is:

K>I>S>S> (Keep It Super Simple)

I don't like having too many things going on at one time.

I like to have time to **FOCUS** on the job at hand.

So, I can aspire to do the 'perfect job' efficiently.

I don't know how you feel about this, we all think and feel different, it is just my point of view.

Please check out the next excerpt, an abstract from an interesting article:

> **"The Negative Effects of Music Videos on our Children**
>
> by *Mon* October 6, 2010 in *GENERAL, MEDIA STUDIES, SOCIETY* with **COMMENTS OFF ON THE NEGATIVE EFFECTS OF MUSIC VIDEOS ON OUR CHILDREN**
>
> ### Abstract:
>
> Several studies indicate a correlation between music videos and violent behavior of adolescents. The findings also show a connection between the imagery displayed in the videos and inappropriate sexual attitudes and conduct. The lyrics tend to have a significant corrupting influence on the youth. Particular genres such as hip-hop, gangsta rap and heavy

metal are found to be more damaging to children than the rest. The racial attitudes and interpersonal relations of teenagers can be influenced by the music they watch." [13]

Need I say more.

Kindly check out the next abstract, let me know what you think and how you feel about it.

Please, I am all ears:

Revised 98(6):1219

A Statement of Retirement for This Policy Was Published At

Paediatrics

November 2009, VOLUME 124 / ISSUE 5
FROM THE AMERICAN ACADEMY OF PEDIATRICS

Impact of Music, Music Lyrics, and Music Videos on Children and Youth

Council on Communications and Media

Abstract

Music plays an important role in the socialization of children and adolescents. Popular music is present

---

[13] http://jottedlines.com/society/the-negative-effects-of-music-videos-on-our-children/ accessed 13th Jan 2018 @ 18:45

almost everywhere, and it is easily available through the radio, various recordings, the Internet, and new technologies allowing adolescents to hear it in diverse settings and situations, alone or shared with friends. Parents often are unaware of the lyrics to which their children are listening because of the increasing use of downloaded music and headphones. Research on popular music has explored its effects on schoolwork, social interactions, mood and affect, and particularly behavior. The effect that popular music has on children's and adolescents' behavior and emotions is of paramount concern. Lyrics have become more explicit in their references to drugs, sex, and violence over the years, particularly in certain genres. A teenager's preference for certain types of music could be correlated or associated with certain behaviors. As with popular music, the perception and the effect of music-video messages are important, because research has reported that exposure to violence, sexual messages, sexual stereotypes, and use of substances of abuse in music videos might produce significant changes in behaviors and attitudes of young viewers. Pediatricians and parents should be aware of this information. Furthermore, with the evidence portrayed in these studies, it is essential for pediatricians and parents to take a stand regarding music lyrics.

music / lyrics / music videos / adolescents / violence"[14]

Let's see what Douglas Gentile from BabyCenter says:

---

14 http://pediatrics.aappublications.org/content/124/5/1488 accessed 13th Jan 2019 @ 18:56

"Is listening to negative lyrics or "angry" music really harmful for my child?"

Douglas Gentile

Developmental Psychologist

Yes—although, surprisingly, the sound of the music has more impact than the lyrics. One study examined how different kinds of music affected the levels of anger and attitudes toward women in teenaged children. Three groups of kids listened to different types of music and lyrics: heavy-metal music with violent lyrics, heavy-metal music with Christian-themed lyrics, and easy-listening music. The kids who listened to heavy metal music, regardless of the lyrical content, developed the same negative attitudes toward women and were more angry than the "easy-listening" kids. (The lyrics of both kinds of heavy metal were actually unintelligible, but the kids assumed the words were about violence and anger because of the accompanying music.)

Why would sound have such a significant effect? One reason is that we all use music for "mood management"—either to get out of a bad mood, for instance or to revel in a given mood (good or bad). If your child and her friends prefer bubble-gum pop music, they're likely to be of a different mindset than kids who listen to, say, gothic rock or pounding heavy-metal music. If your child seems to favor angry-sounding music (children as young as 8 months can discern "angry" musical tones) then you should talk to her—and possibly to a child psychologist—about whether she's feeling anxious and upset a lot and, if so, why. On the other hand, if your child also has a couple of rap or heavy-metal CDs in her collection of mostly pop or country music, then she's probably just experimenting—something kids this age are really good at."[15]

---

15 https://www.babycenter.com/404_is-listening-to-negative-lyrics-or-angry-music-really-harmfu_71171.bc accessed 13th Jan 2019 @ 19:03

Why I Know That You Do Not Love Your Children!

Douglas does share my sentiments here, but many people disagree with this line of thinking. Especially the young, as they often come out with comments such as:

> Wow ok I'm using my mums account to post this.
>
> 1. Heavy metal is a type of music and people read it as some satanic devil exorcism stuff
>
> 2. I am a well-behaved child who loves heavy metal
>
> 3. You do not need a therapist if you like a certain type of music, I have a strong feeling towards this subject that parents are 'scared' in case their child does angry things like the music. If your child is like this then yes, there may be something up. But just listening to a type of music isn't going to hurt your child or damage their brain or make them fail tests
>
> Writing this just in case any mums agree with whatever this is
>
>
>
> a BabyCenter Member
>
> 16th Jul 2015

There are many things in the world today that simply did not exist before.

Just a few years ago, when I was younger, there was no internet or telephone in my world.

There was no Facebook, LinkedIn, Google, Amazon, Tik Tok, Snapchat, or Instagram. There wasn't even email!

The world as I remember it was a much better place.

WE HAD MORE HAPPINESS, LOVE, TIME, MONEY, KNOWLEDGE, AND POWER.

That is what I remember; does anyone else?

What's happening to the world these days?

Sometimes, we are too busy, too stuck, to see the things we should. Our eyes get cloudy, which can lead to the deception of good people.

Let me ask you something. Please, answer honestly, for yourself.

How many times in your life have you been adamant about something, only to be proven wrong later?

Why I Know That You Do Not Love Your Children!

It has happened to me plenty; that's why I never presume knowledge. Facts are forever evolving. I always take my time with things. I've found this is always the quickest way to get things done properly. I think you know that.

Remember, time does not stand still.

Or does it?

You tell me.

Many people seem to know too much, but do they?

Please do not ask me, I am no judge.

I feel that, in order to make the world a better place, we parents must be more aware of the music and entertainment that influence our children.

Our children are our golden ones, and we need to be a little more protective.

CHAPTER 6:
SOCIAL MEDIA ADDICTION

Kwadw(o) Naya: Baa Ankh Em Re A'lyun Eil

"Would You Quit Facebook for $1,000 Per Year? Study Finds Most Wouldn't"

By Troy Thompson January 2, 2019

Credit: Wachiwit / Shutterstock

How much money would it take for you to delete your Facebook account? With the very real and well-documented cases of social media addiction on the rise, even despite the company's recent stint of security snafus and highly-publicized data scandals, the answer for the majority of average users is an amount greater than $1,000 per year.

That's according to the results of a recent PLOS study conducted by researchers with four leading post-secondary institutions, including Sean Cash (Tufts), Saleem Alhabash (MSU), Jay Corrigan, an Economist affiliated with Kenyon College, and his colleague, Matt Rousu, of Pennsylvania's Susquehanna University.

How Much Is Social Media Worth?

In their extensive report, dubbed "How much is social media worth? Estimating the value of Facebook by paying users to stop using it," the researchers not only reveal how hard it is for users to actually give up using the social media platform but suggest that users would, "on average," not stop using their Facebook account altogether if given a nominal daily cash incentive.

"Though the populations sampled and the auction design differ across the experiments, we consistently find the average Facebook user would require more than $1,000 to deactivate their account for one year," the researchers claimed, ultimately concluding that while Facebook's impact on the economy may be minimal, its perceived value, to the majority of its users, is still quite high."[16]

I came across this article today and I felt it was a little worrying, as it just highlights the level of social media addiction today.

---

16 https://www.idropnews.com/news/fast-tech/would-you-quit-facebook-for-1000-per-year-study-finds-most-wouldnt/90472/?utm_source=tapp&utm_medium=tapp&utm_campaign=tapp010419&utm_term=tapp accessed 14th Jan 2019 @ 06:22

Social media addiction is a phrase that we do not often hear which is pretty surprising considering the eco platforms and applications that we have at our disposal such as:

- Facebook
- Linked In
- Instagram
- Snapchat
- Twitter
- Google Hangouts
- WhatsApp
- BBM (Blackberry Messenger)
- We Chat
- Line
- Viber
- Tango
- Kik
- Facetime
- Skype
- Telegram
- Voxer
- Hey Tel

- Talkatone
- MySpace
- Reddit
- Telegram
- Foursquare
- DeviantArt
- Flickr
- Quora
- Discord
- TikTok
- Twitch
- Soundcloud
- Medium
- Vimeo
- Giphy
- Imgur

- Clubhouse
- WeChat
- Tumblr
- Baidu Tieba
- Sina Weibo
- VKontakte (VK)
- Pinterest

Which consume so much of our daily lives.

Social media is great, I do agree but it is easy to abuse. It interferes with our daily lives.

At present, there is no official medical recognition of social media addiction as a disease or a disorder, but it is something parents need to remain vigilant about.

Social networking has changed the way we communicate, do business, get our daily news fix. and so much more. Our lives have most definitely improved as we have become more connected.

But what is the downside to all of this technology?

We are incredibly distracted these days!

We need to be at least as good as our children when it comes to keeping up with apps and gadgetry. So we know what harm these things could be doing.

It depends on who you talk to and how your children are using social media. A site like Facebook could serve as a launchpad for a new business owner or it could be an inescapable source of negative peer pressure for a young teen. There is also the addiction factor to consider. How much time do I spend on Facebook? How much time does my daughter? That is what I need to consider. Then there is also the security and tracking issues that we face with all this new technology. They always seem to be asking for permission to record our data, track us, and obtain information on our habits or whereabouts. Have you ever noticed?

Pretty worrying if you ask me, but it is just my humble opinion.

It is great that we now have many forms of instant communication. It is also great that we have instant news courtesy of the internet and social media, but what about the misinformation, distraction, and addiction?

Social media can be great for business, entertainment, and recreation but it can be very detrimental as many of us know.

What are the cons, you may ask?

That is a very good question; I will list some:

- Information overload
- Privacy issues
- Social peer pressure and cyberbullying
- Online interaction substituted for offline interaction.
- Distraction and procrastination
- Sedentary lifestyle habits and sleep disruption

When we break things down like this, it's very easy to see how social media can come into play. I see it day in, day out. Often, I see people spending more time online than they do off.

Have you seen it?

I have a cousin who lives on Facebook. She says that Facebook is her boyfriend, I kid you not.

In fact, most of my younger cousins' lives are consumed by Facebook, Snapchat, and Instagram. They even use these things when they are driving. I have seen it and I am sure you have too.

What do you think about all of this?

People are distracted from their real lives by social media?.

Let me ask you something.

How often do you see someone look at their phone?

How often do you see people getting distracted by social media apps, the news, and messages that they receive? This leads to all sorts of problems.

I am sure I am not the only one that has seen this?

Browsing social media can also feed procrastination habits and become something people turn to in order to avoid responsibilities. People these days are addicted to spending hours and hours and hours online, doing meaningless tasks. Communication has become easier, it's undeniable. But, what is also undeniable, is the fact that we have become lazier, more useless, and generally dumber than our ancestors. This is most alarming! Things are meant to be getting better, not worse.

We are in the information age, we have to face it and deal with it. I also know that there is no room for dinosaurs; they went extinct a long time ago. We need to roll with the new age.

That is all I have to say really. I would just like to leave you with one extract to peruse:

"Social media addiction is a bigger problem than you think"

Can't stay away from social media? You're not alone; social networking is engineered to be as habit-forming as crack cocaine.

Social networks are massively addictive. Most people I know check and interact on social sites constantly throughout the day. And they have no idea how much actual time they spend on social media.

If you're a social media addict, and your addiction is getting worse, there's a reason for that: most of the major social network companies, as well as social content creators, are working hard every day to make their networks so addictive that you can't resist them.

By Mike Elgan

Contributing Columnist, Computerworld | DEC 14, 2015 3:11 **AM PT**"[17]

---

17 https://www.computerworld.com/article/3014439/internet/social-media-addiction-is-a-bigger-problem-than-you-think.html accessed 14th Jan 2019 @ 07:54

CHAPTER 7A: RELATIONSHIPS

What do we teach our children about relationships?

And at what age?

I am not talking about sex.

I am talking about relationships.

Our children are not our personal property or possessions.

One day, they may decide to leave the family home to make one of their own.

This is life as it should be.

But, is it?

It wasn't for me. My parents split up before I was even a teenager, and my father moved far away. I was thrown out of my family home at the age of 15, never to return.

I was not taught about relationships. I had to work things out.

I thought it was a good idea, like any young man around me, to have as many girlfriends as possible. It was all a game for bragging rights.

How silly is that?

Nobody told us different.

I really, really wish that I had more knowledge.

The **RIGHT KNOWLEDGE**, the **RIGHT WISDOM**, which would have given me the **RIGHT UNDERSTANDING**, which would have led to 'GOOD' LOGIC and SOUND 'RIGHT' REASONING.

I have a daughter and I would never like to see any of this happen to her.

But this is the world around us, and it seems to be getting worse with the overuse of technology.

Are long lasting relationships the norm in this day and age?

I think we should teach our children forbidden knowledge. Things like peace, unity, and togetherness. Things they don't know about life, **afterlife, reproduction, and evolution.**

Life isn't something you can just **YOLO**.

What do you think?

Can you imagine a world where people only set out to find the one they will marry? Where they have babies together, that they nurture, guide, support, love, and raise them to have babies that can do the same?

That is the nature of nature.

Wouldn't that be a better way to go?

What do you think?

CHAPTER 7B: SEX

I was hesitant to cover this topic, because it's so personal. But, they go hand in hand don't they.

What is a relationship without sex?

You tell me.

When should we talk to our children about sex?

Before they have it, but I am no expert.

What do we tell our children about sex?

I cannot answer this question for every parent, that's not my place.

I am no child expert.

I am just a 'bad' father who is trying to be a better one.

I think we need to **TEACH OUR CHILDREN** how **SACRED** sex is and how it needs to be **RESPECTED**.

We need to teach them the dangers of having indiscriminate sex, that there are sexual predators, and there exists a point to having sex.

I don't feel that sex should just be for personal pleasure.

I know there's more to it than that.

I wish i never had sex until I was married.

I would have loved to have gotten married at 16-18 years old, and I would love to have spent many years having sex and pleasure in a lasting, loving relationship that brought good children into the world.

But instead, I had many, many, many short-term and non-relationships.

I have never been in a relationship that has lasted longer than 3 years, but I have a child. I'm saying this because I know I didn't do it in the right order. I want my next relationship to be my last one

Doesn't a wife or husband sound better than a girlfriend/boyfriend or **LINK** or **FWB** (f*ck with buddy) or even the good old **friends with benefits** or **FB's** (F*ck Buddies)?

I know many of you will not like reading this.

Some may think that Kwadw(o) Naya: Baa Ankh Em Re A'lyun Eil is a raving idiot.

If this is the case, I am very sorry, but this is just the way I feel, I do not mean to offend anybody.

The world we live in has been dominated by negative sexual energies, that I know. Don't believe me? Check it out for yourself.

What are we going to do?

CHAPTER 8:
LIES

"Mwannesi Wade"

7 January at 16:41

Thank you to all family, friends and associates who helped make it a great birthday!!!

It's now 2019, and I have so many unanswered questions..

I haven't found out who let the dogs out...where's the beef...how to get to Sesame Street or why all flavors of Fruit Loops taste exactly the same. And how many licks does it take to get to the center of a Tootsie Pop...... why are eggs packed in a flimsy carton, but batteries are secured in plastic that's tough as nails... why "abbreviated" is such a long word; or why there's a D in 'fridge' but not in refrigerator...

Why lemon juice is made with artificial flavor yet dish-washing liquid is made with real lemons... why they sterilize the needle for lethal injections... and why do you "put your two cents in" yet it's only a "penny for your thoughts" (where's that extra penny going)... why do The Alphabet Song and Twinkle Twinkle Little Star have the same tune... why did you just try to sing those two previous songs... and just what exactly is Victoria's secret? And where is Wally?... Can you hear me now?...And do you really think I am this witty??

I actually got this piece from a friend, who stole it from her brother's girlfriend's, uncle's cousin who lived next door to an old classmate's mailman...Now it's your turn to take it from me...

Copy and Paste and enjoy your day. ☺ ☺

Thanks again for a great birthday!"[18]

---

[18] https://www.facebook.com/nes.wade accessed 16th Jan 2019 @ 21:32

I saw this post today from my Facebook friend Mwannesi Wade and it inspired me to write this chapter. The thought was actually in my head a few days ago but this post triggered off an explosion in my brain.

How many times are we treated like **mushrooms** by our parents?

What is a mushroom you may ask?

MUSHROOM

> "A mushroom, or toadstool, is the fleshy, spore-bearing, fruiting body of a fungus, typically produced above ground on soil or on its food source."[19]

It was not a trick question. We all should know what a mushroom is.

Then why do our parents treat us this way? I don't get it.

I don't understand!

I don't innerstand.

And I also don't overstand?

You see, when I was younger. even to this day, my mother and father have done nothing but lie to me.

Yes, you heard me right, they **LIED** to me.

And believe me, I could use a much stronger word for what they did.

---

[19] https://en.wikipedia.org/wiki/Mushroom accessed 17th Jan 2019 @ 06:25

Why I Know That You Do Not Love Your Children!

Most parents LIE to their children! I am sure you've experienced this.

I am sure most of you will agree.

Do you think I love my parents for this?

Or that I hate them?

They lost love from me, of course, which is very sad because I am sure they were trying. They are good people.

But they lost respect from me.

And I am sorry, Mum and Dad, but I am not afraid to admit it.

Do you mind if I ask you a question?

What is the hardest thing to gain and the easiest thing to lose?

TRUST!

Do you think I still trust my parents?

They are very nice people, always smiling, always seeming to care for me. But, they damaged me by lying constantly.

Now, it's incredibly difficult for me to relate to Mummy and Daddy. I think that they are crazy or maybe even 'sleeping'. This is probably the reason I left home at age 15.

How could they do this to me and still claim to **LOVE** me?

I don't get it.

Would you like to hear something funny?

They think I'm the crazy one!

Yes, you heard right.

I don't know, I guess we are on different frequencies.

I don't really want to say too much but I will give you an example of some of the lies.

I am still hurt today because the tooth fairy doesn't come anymore whenever I **lose teeth**. I used to look forward to that.

Christmas comes, and Santa doesn't bring me presents anymore. I do not get to sit on the nice old man's lap and hear those nice words and get those nice gifts? (I guess that pleasantry is only for our children). My parents never did tell me the true meaning of Christmas, and when I found out, I was devasted, as you can imagine.

They never told me about Easter and the sex rituals, or explained about the Easter eggs and people f*cking like rabbits? (Please excuse my French!).

They lied to me about my nationality, told me nothing about my predecessors.

I remember always hearing things like this from my mother, father and some other elders when I was younger

There is one good thing that we were taught and that is to respect our elders. That Pearl of wisdom was ingrained in me for **LIFE** and I really do **LOVE** my Mummy and Daddy for teaching me that. Now that is **DIVINE LOVE**.

I also remember them saying things like:

- Drink your milk, it will make you big and strong (*I no longer drink milk as I found out that animal milk is no good for human consumption*).

- If you tell the truth you will not get in trouble
  (*How gullible was I when I was younger? Wouldn't it be better for them to tell me to always be responsible for my own actions as the truth often hurts?*).

I am sure that you can see where I am coming from.

I really like these Mummy and Daddy people but, to this day they still treated me like a **MUSHROOM**, even though I tried to advise them otherwise.

Let me share my thoughts with you:

> "Mummy and Daddy, why are you always lying to me? Do you know that's not very nice? Do you also know that it hurts me very deeply when you act this way?
>
> This has happened through out my life, all this pain and torture it has even made me doubt myself.
>
> When I was younger, I used to feel so **GODLY**, now I feel so angry and confused.
>
> Mum and Dad, why have you done this to me?
>
> Oh why, oh why, oh why?

There was a time when I found it difficult to take heed to any advice that was given to me by my good elders. I had been lied to so much by the ones I loved. If the lovers are going to lie to me, what's going to happen when I meet haters. What are they going to tell me?

I realise now that almost everything those good old elders taught me was a lie.

Thanks Mother and Father!

> How can you expect me to listen to you now?
>
> Maybe you need to ask yourself.
>
> But I do not blame you. I both **OVER**stand and innerstand a great deal of the **KNOW-LEDGE** that you had in your possession.
>
> Did you not realise that I have been eaten up with self-doubt most of life? Until I could decipher the **GODLY** from the devilish?
>
> Distrusting the world around me has opened my eyes.
>
> Did you know that when parents tell a child something they know is not true? They cause their child to choose between trusting themselves and trusting their parents.
>
> Surely, a child is meant to trust their parents?
>
> Mummy, Daddy, I'm not stupid. I was born with common sense.
>
> I am sorry, but these are words I had to say. I have been trying to **SHOW YOU ALL**, to explain life, so that no other youngster has to go through the same things.

Do you think anyone will listen to me?

Kwadw(o) Naya: Baa Ankh Em Re A'lyun Eil is crazy again!

What's up with this world?

What's wrong with you? I get it now, I was the problem all along

You see mushrooms get kept in the dark and feed on excrement.

Seems comparable to the world we live in now, doesn't it?

No wonder the rich are getting richer and the poor are getting poorer.

MUSHROOMISM NEEDS TO STOP!

I really do have **DIVINE LOVE** for my parents. I **LOVE** them dearly, despite what they put me through.

Or maybe I put them through a lot?

WHO KNOWS?

CHAPTER 9: RELIGION

I don't usually talk about religion; it is a very sensitive, personal thing.

I feel it's time too now.

I am not religious or anti-religious.

Here, religion is all we know

And there are so many!

With this in mind, I would like to say one thing:

In order to escape **'THE MATRIX'** and **FREE OURSELVES** from the shackles imposed on us. It is vital that we create a spiritual reality of our own. That we transcend the collective human generative path of ego, emotion, and mind, which is so often ruled by programming.

I see a lot of bloodshed in the world today, caused by personal beliefs. Have you seen it?

I feel that, regardless of whatever beliefs we have, that we all respect the backgrounds, cultures and beliefs of others accordingly. It is the only way.

Everyone was brought up differently and we are all from different cultures. Of course, we are going to believe different things, but it doesn't mean that we have to have negative beliefs. Nor does it mean that we have to fight, argue, or kill for our beliefs.

WHAT DO YOU THINK?

Yet there are wars, fights, and arguments throughout the globe, day in and day out.

Can **YOU** see it?

This is not necessary.

It is simple!

We just need to teach our children differently.

That is all.

THEY ARE THE NEW WORLD.

And this is a fact.

What type of new world are we going to **CREATE?**

I **LOVE EVERYTHING** about **RIGHTEOUSNESS**, and this is **RIGHTEOUS**. I am sure you will agree.

CONCLUSION

What is the **TRUTH** of this world?

This is something I ask myself every single day. Why is it the information that is fed to us by society, our parents, and the media, untrue? Why are we spun a web of lies? What is the government trying to cover up? What are they trying to hide?

It appears that, throughout our lives, we are constantly lied to. Our parents lie to us in childhood and the media lies to us as adults. We remain distracted and preoccupied by technology and social media, which take up most of our lives and provide a false idea that we are free. In reality, we are less free and worse off in comparison to the freedom of our ancestors. Why are we being programmed like robots?

Why are our lives being dictated to us? Why are our children being indoctrinated by music and entertainment seeped in so much aggression and violence? Why are we constantly being reminded of the divisions in society? Why aren't we teaching our children unity and world peace? Are we living in a dictatorship?

Why does the popular culture of today include teenagers having as many partners as possible? Why does it matter how many people you sleep with on a night out? Why is the number of sexual partners you have a status symbol? We should teach our children traditional values and the meaning of true love and the purpose of sex.

Only when we find the truth will we be able to live free and prosperous lives. This is how we will encourage the younger generation to make good decisions based on true knowledge, ensuring the future of our world.

ACKNOWLEDGEMENTS

I would like to give **GREAT THANKS AND ACKNOWLEDGEMENTS** to the people who helped me bring this work to fruition:

BIG THANKS to Hayley Jukes and Aspivey5 for their magnificent editorial works, Stephen from Expert Designs for the book cover and a very **LARGE** thanks to Akinsola Olayinka from **HANSBARROW CREATIVES** not only for his diligence and patience but for the **EXCELLENT** job he did with the formatting under very difficult circumstances, many others may have failed.

THANK YOU ALL once again, with out **YOU ALL** it would not be possible.

THANKS AND ACKNOWLEDGEMENT to **ALL READING** this **WITHOUT YOU** there would be **NO POINT**.

PEACE and LOVE FAMILY!

AFTERWORD

Thank you once again for being with me. It is always such a pleasure. Please look out for Scroll 3, it will be out very soon. We'll speak again soon.

Love and best wishes!

Kwadw(o) Naya: Baa Ankh Em Re A'lyun Eil

onlygold@goldenchildpromotionspublishing.gold

https://goldenchildpromotionspublishing.gold/

http://kwadwonayabaaankhemrealyuneil.gold

If you enjoyed this book, why don't you try the next instalment:

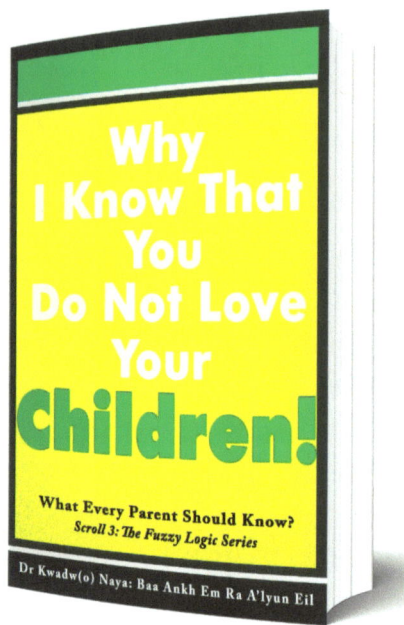

Pre-order it now at the link below for only **$1.30** usually it is **$7**.

https://goldenchildpromotionspublishing.gold/product-category/why-i-know-that-you-do-not-love-your-children-series/why-i-know-that-you-do-not-love-your-children-scroll3/

Don't delay, when the time is gone it is gone!!!

ABOUT THE AUTHOR

Kwadw(o) Naya: Baa Ankh Em Re A'lyun Eil

Born: Catterick Garrison, UK

Nationality: British

Race: Autochthonous Carbonite

Genre: Non-Fiction

Notable awards: A Masters in Business as well as many other vocational qualifications.

Kwadw(o) Naya: Baa Ankh Em Re A'lyun Eil is an Author, Director, Mentor and Life Coach ('Transformational'), he is a new gentleman on the scene, one of the most promising newcomers for 2019.

He was born in a country where he has never been accepted, raised in a broken povertystricken home, which he was thrown out at the age of 15 never to return. Surprisingly he has had a very good career, **NOT GREAT**, and is educated to master's level with 'degrees' in street knowledge. Despite his successes there has always been some unseen **FORCES** working against him, which he is only too happy to share.

Somehow, he has excelled with everything that he has touched and is not afraid of **CHANGE**, moving from running his own estate agency in the capital city of London (UK) to becoming a fully established author, mentor and life coach.

Kwadw(o) Naya: Baa Ankh Em Re A'lyun Eil is ready to share his **KNOWLEDGE, WISDOM,** and **OVERSTANDING** with **YOU ALL**.

He has written 25 books to date, please watch out for his works.

www.ingramcontent.com/pod-product-compliance
Lightning Source LLC
Chambersburg PA
CBHW040159100526
44590CB00001B/7